# Fisher-Price® PRESCHOOL WORKBOOK

## FUN WITH LEARNING

MODERN PUBLISHING
A Division of Unisystems, Inc.
New York, New York 10022
Series UPC #49680

# NOTE TO PARENTS

Dear Parents:

Helping your children master their world through early learning is as easy as the Fisher-Price® Workbooks!

As your child's first and most important teacher, you can encourage your child's love of learning by participating in learning activities at home. Working together on the activities in each of the Fisher-Price® Preschool Workbooks will help your child build confidence, learn to reason, and develop reading, writing, math, and language skills.

Help make your time together enjoyable and rewarding by following these suggestions:

- Choose a quiet time when you and your child are relaxed, and not tired.
- Provide a selection of writing materials (pens, pencils, or crayons).
- Discuss each page. Help your child relate the concepts in the books to everyday experiences.
- Only work on a few pages at a time. Don't attempt to complete every page if your child becomes tired or loses interest.
- Praise your child's efforts.


Fisher-Price® Preschool Workbook titles:

- EXPLORING MY WORLD
- I CAN LEARN
- LET'S FIND OUT
- READY FOR SCHOOL
- FUN WITH LEARNING
- GETTING STARTED
- ON THE ROAD TO LEARNING
- WATCH ME LEARN

# ESSENTIAL SKILLS

Each chapter contains repetitive activities that have been designed to help children learn to sort, separate, put together, and develop the organizational skills necessary for learning and thinking.

## Chapter 1  It's Fun to Think and Do

Visual discrimination activities, such as looking for details, noticing likenesses and differences, and continuing patterns, are included, along with some activities that promote critical thinking, fine motor skill development, association, and classification skills.

## Chapter 2  It's Fun to Learn New Words

This chapter features pages that develop concepts for specific words, such as *right, left,* and *middle.* Opposites, numbers and number words, colors, and shape words are also included. The words taught are highlighted so that your early reader can focus attention on them.

## Chapter 3  It's Fun to Begin Writing

Tracing vertical lines, horzintal lines, and curves is presented within the context of play. There are also pages for children to practice writing the upper- and lowercase letters of the alphabet. Recognizing letter order and practicing letter sounds and words help children continue to build listening and language skills.

## Chapter 4  It's Fun to Work with Numbers

Activities teach beginning math concepts, including counting numbers, counting to fifty to recognize number order, creating and matching sets, and making comparisons to understand more, less, and zero.

# TABLE OF CONTENTS

# IT'S FUN TO THINK AND DO

Can you fix the car?
Circle the two pictures that are exactly the same.

**Skills**: Recognizing differences; Noticing details

# IT'S FUN TO THINK AND DO

What a big mouth he has!
Circle the two whales that are exactly the same.

**Skills**: Recognizing differences; Noticing details

# IT'S FUN TO THINK AND DO

Look at each row of pictures.
Something is missing from one picture.
Circle that picture.

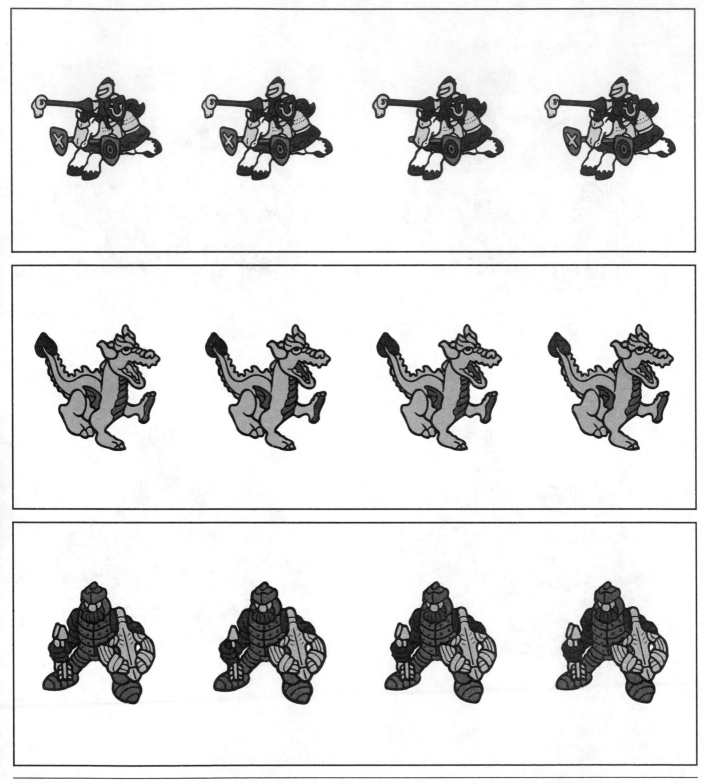

**Skills**: Visual discrimination; Noticing details

# IT'S FUN TO THINK AND DO

Look at each row of pictures.
Something is missing from one picture.
Circle that picture.

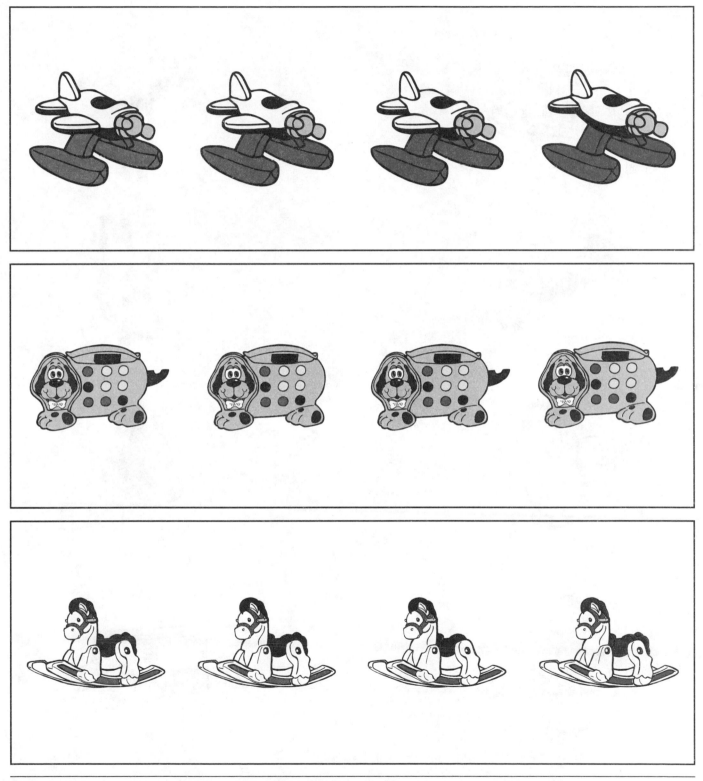

**Skills**: Visual discrimination; Noticing details

# IT'S FUN TO THINK AND DO

Look at the pictures on this page.
Draw a line to connect the pictures that match.

**Skills**: Association; Visual discrimination

# IT'S FUN TO THINK AND DO

Look at the pictures on this page.
Draw a line to connect the pictures that match.

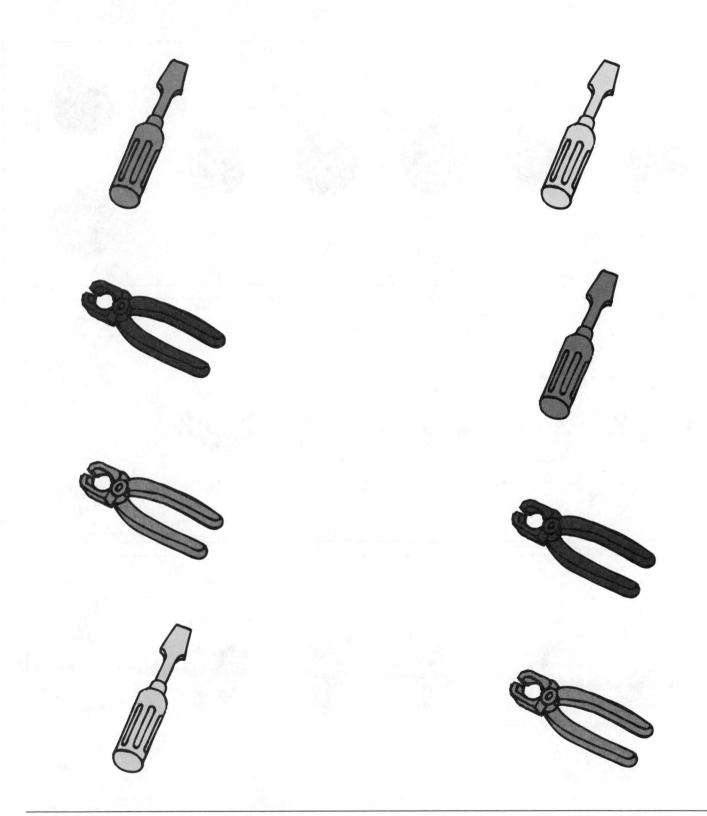

**Skills**: Association; Visual discrimination

# IT'S FUN TO THINK AND DO

Look at the pattern in each row.
Draw a circle around the picture
that continues each pattern.

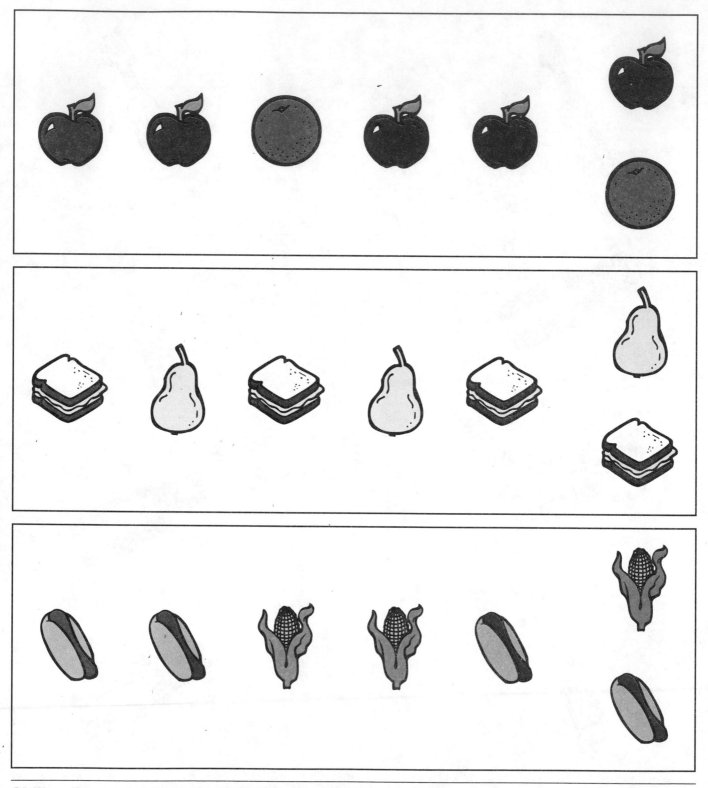

**Skills**: Observing and continuing patterns; Visual memory

# IT'S FUN TO THINK AND DO

Look at the pattern in each row.
Draw a circle around the picture
that continues each pattern.

**Skills**: Observing and continuing patterns; Visual memory

# IT'S FUN TO THINK AND DO

Lemonade for sale! Lemonade!
Help the girl get to the lemonade stand.

START

FINISH

**Skills**: Visual perception; Fine motor skill development

# IT'S FUN TO THINK AND DO

Drawing with chalk is so much fun!
Help the girl get back to her hopscotch game.

START

FINISH

1 2 3 4 5 6

**Skills**: Visual perception; Fine motor skill development

# IT'S FUN TO THINK AND DO

Look closely at each row of pictures.
One of the pictures is in a different position.
Put an **X** on that picture.

**Skills**: Spatial orientation; Noticing details

# IT'S FUN TO THINK AND DO

Look at the pictures in each row.
Put an **X** on the one that does not belong.
Tell why it doesn't belong.

**Skills**: Association; Classification; Logical reasoning

# IT'S FUN TO THINK AND DO

Look at the pictures in each row.
Put an **X** on the one that does not belong.
Tell why it doesn't belong.

**Skills**: Association; Classification; Logical reasoning

# IT'S FUN TO THINK AND DO

Look at the pictures in each row.
Put an **X** on the one that does not belong.
Tell why it doesn't belong.

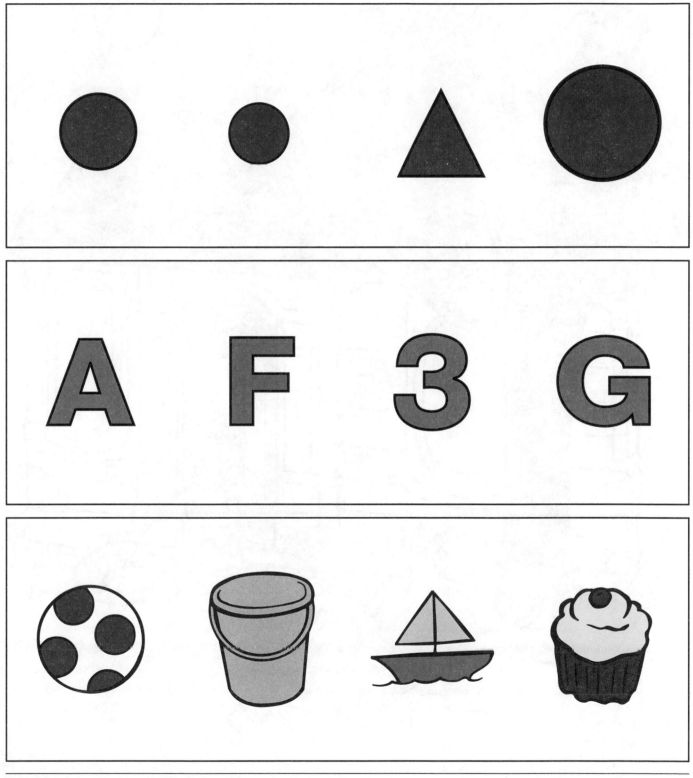

**Skills**: Association; Classification; Logical reasoning

# IT'S FUN TO THINK AND DO

What's wrong with this picture?
Find four wrong things.
Put an **X** on each one.

**Skills**: Logical reasoning; Noticing details

# IT'S FUN TO THINK AND DO

What's wrong with this picture?
Find five wrong things.
Put an **X** on each one.

**Skills**: Logical reasoning; Noticing details

# IT'S FUN TO LEARN NEW WORDS

Look closely at each row of Little People®.
One of them in each row is facing **left**.
Circle that one.

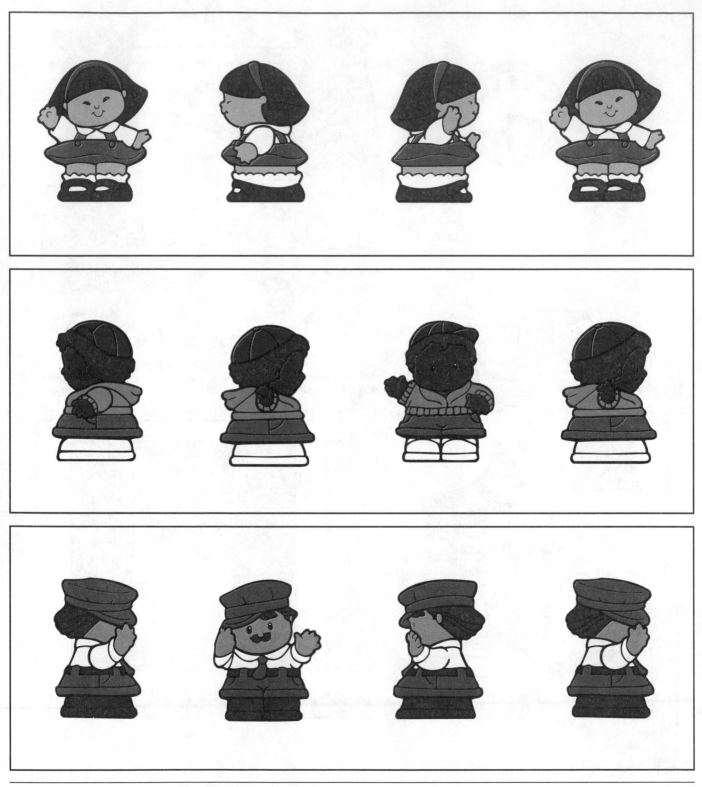

**Skills**: Spatial orientation; Noticing details; Building vocabulary

# IT'S FUN TO LEARN NEW WORDS

Look closely at each row of animals.
One of the animals in each row is facing **right**.
Put an **X** on that animal.

**Skills**: Spatial orientation; Noticing details; Building vocabulary

# IT'S FUN TO LEARN NEW WORDS

Which one is in the **middle**?
Look at the Little People® in each row.
Circle the one that is in the **middle**.

**Skills**: Spatial orientation; Noticing details; Building vocabulary

# IT'S FUN TO LEARN NEW WORDS

Look at the pictures.
Tell where the people and animals are.
Then draw the lines to connect the opposites.

**in**            **out**

---

**Skills**: Recognizing opposites; Building vocabulary

# IT'S FUN TO LEARN NEW WORDS

Look at the pictures.
Tell whether you see the **front** or **back** of the people or things.
Then draw lines to connect the opposites.

## front                                    back

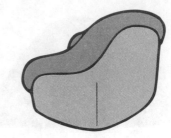

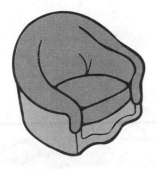

---

**Skills**: Recognizing opposites; Building vocabulary

# IT'S FUN TO LEARN NEW WORDS

Look at the first shape in each row and say its name.
Next, trace the dotted shape.
Then draw the shape. What color will you make it?

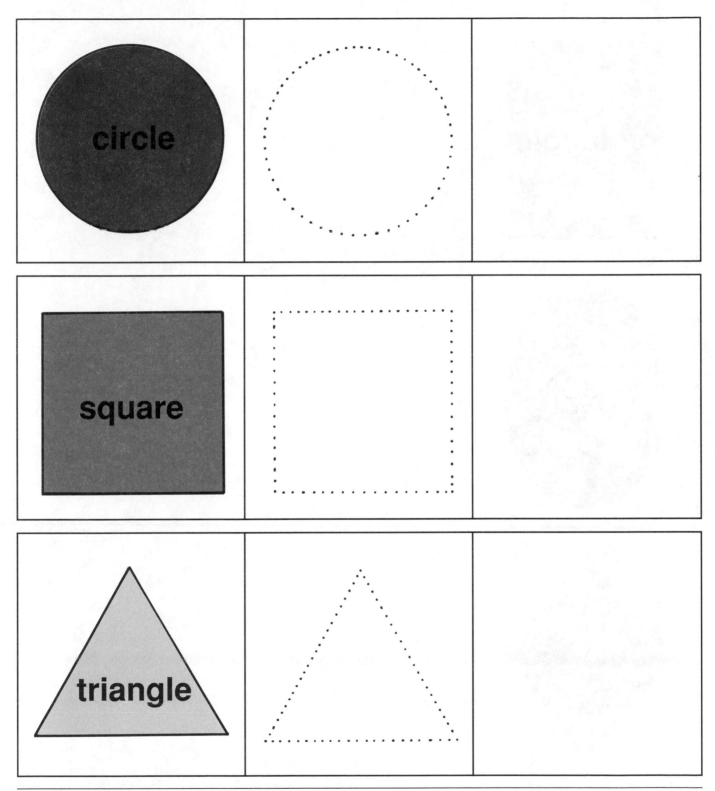

**Skills**: Recognizing shapes; Building vocabulary; Developing small motor control

# IT'S FUN TO LEARN NEW WORDS

Look at the first shape in each row and say its name.
Next, trace the dotted shape.
Then draw the shape. What color will you make it?

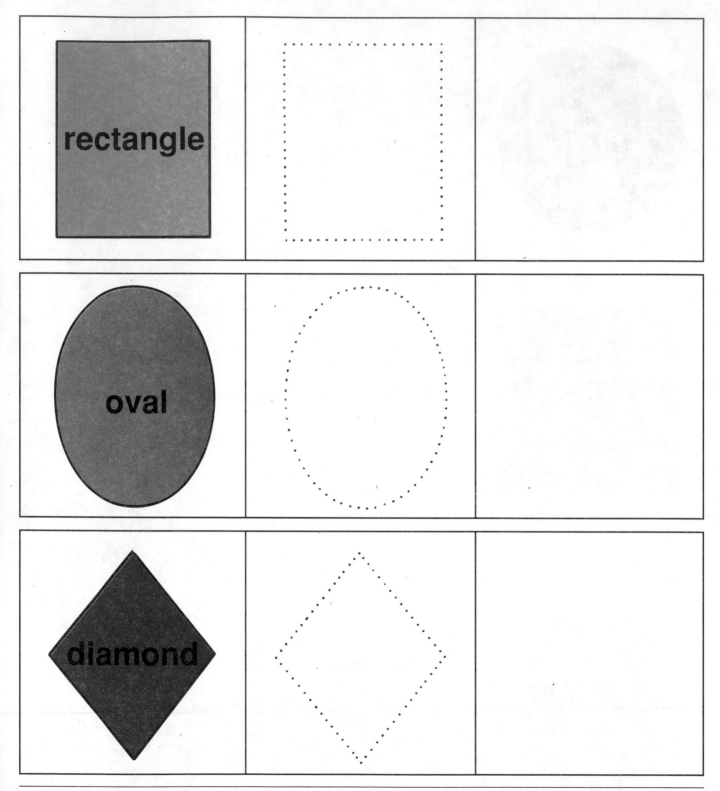

**Skills**: Recognizing shapes; Building vocabulary; Developing small motor control

# IT'S FUN TO LEARN NEW WORDS

Look at each number and count its set of pictures.
Next, read each word and count its set of pictures.
Then draw lines to connect each number to its number word.

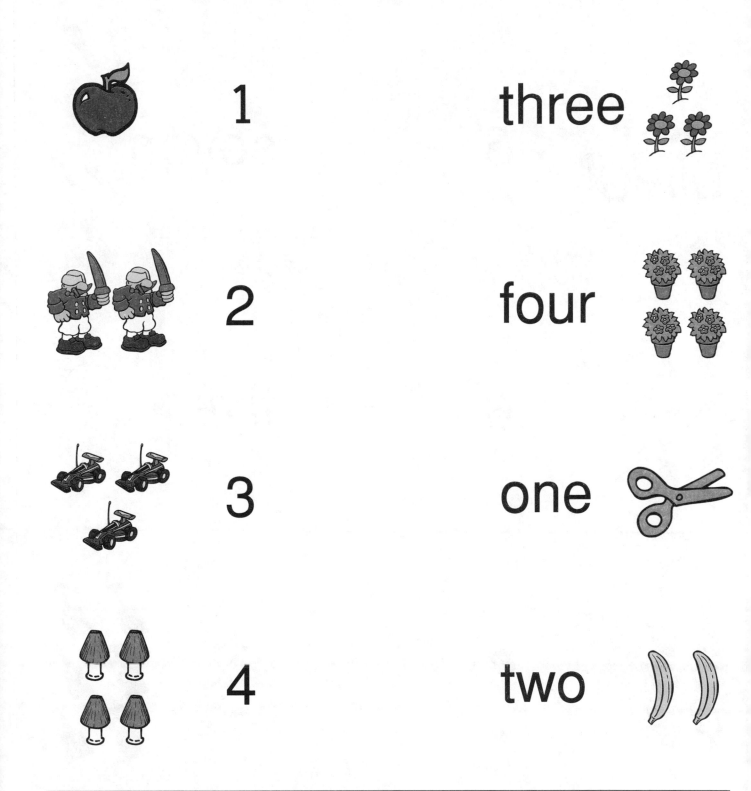

**Skills**: Counting; Recognizing numbers; Building vocabulary

# IT'S FUN TO LEARN NEW WORDS

Look at each number and count its set of pictures.
Next, read each word and count its set of pictures.
Then draw lines to connect each number to its number word.

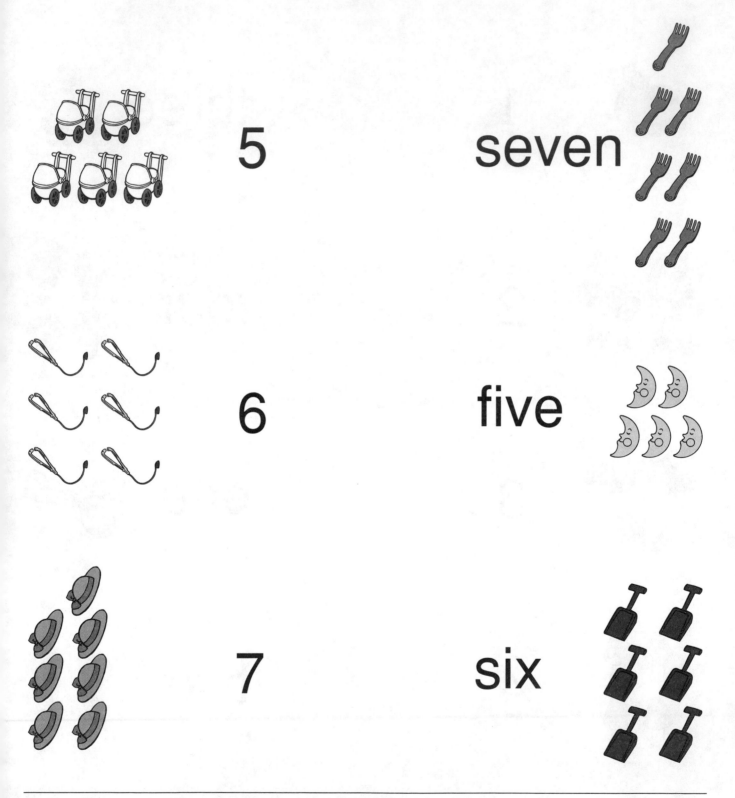

5

seven

6

five

7

six

**Skills:** Counting; Recognizing numbers; Building vocabulary

# IT'S FUN TO LEARN NEW WORDS

Look at each number and count its set of pictures.
Next, read each word and count its set of pictures.
Then draw lines to connect each number to its number word.

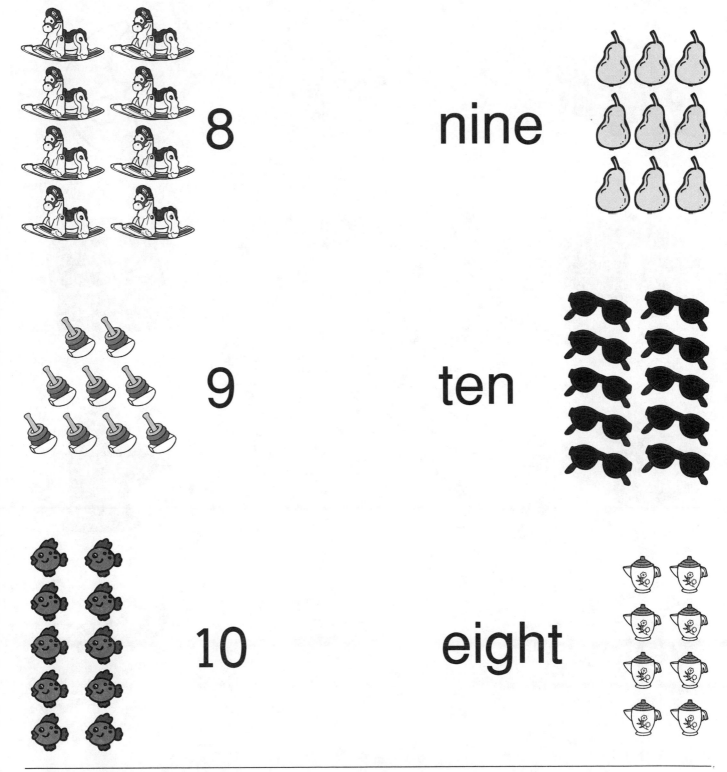

---

**Skills**: Counting; Recognizing numbers; Building vocabulary

# IT'S FUN TO LEARN NEW WORDS

Look at each color and say its name.
Then draw lines to connect each color word to its matching toy.

 red

 green

 blue

yellow

---

**Skills**: Recognizing colors; Building vocabulary

# IT'S FUN TO LEARN NEW WORDS

Look at each color and say its name.
Then draw lines to connect each color word to its matching toy.

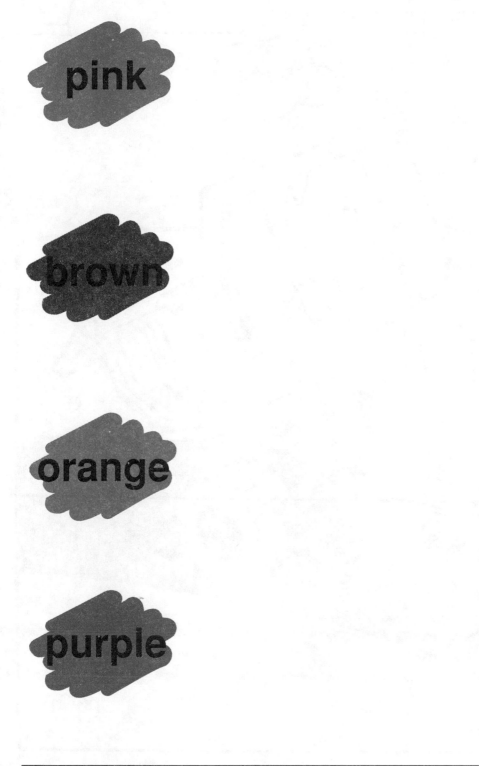

pink

brown

orange

purple

**Skills**: Recognizing colors; Building vocabulary

# IT'S FUN TO LEARN NEW WORDS

Color the **Y** spaces **yellow**.
Color the **R** spaces **red**.
Color the **B** spaces **blue**.
Color the **G** spaces **green**.
Leave all the other spaces white.
Then you'll know what you can use to carry heavy loads.

**Skills:** Identifying colors

# IT'S FUN TO BEGIN WRITING

Bring the objects together.
Start at the dots.
Trace the broken lines.

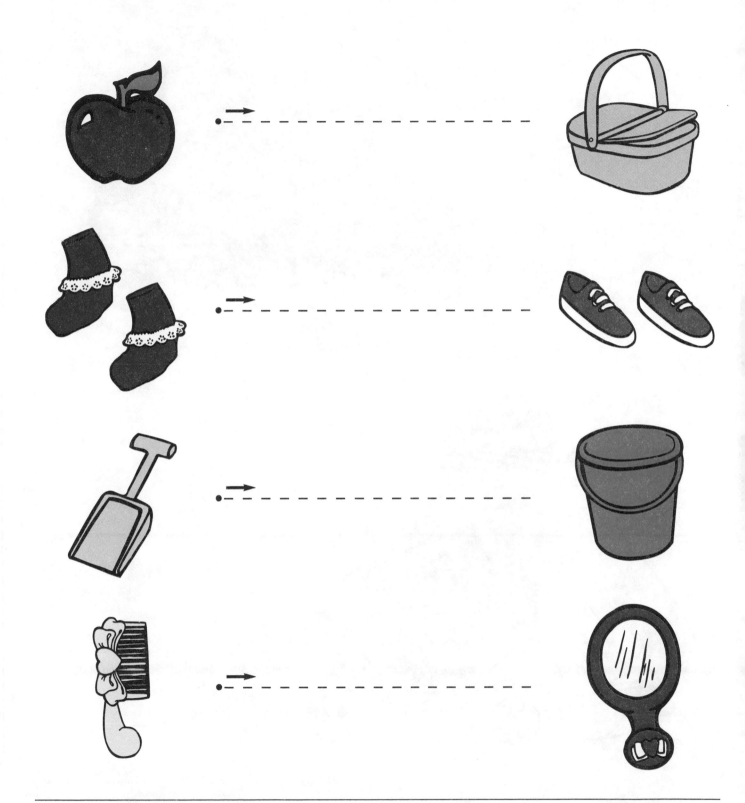

**Skills**: Fine motor skill development; Eye/hand coordination; Forming horizontal lines

# IT'S FUN TO BEGIN WRITING

Finish the wheels.
Start at the dots.
Trace the broken lines.
Then watch them go!

**Skills**: Fine motor skill development; Eye/hand coordination; Forming closed curves

# IT'S FUN TO BEGIN WRITING

Help them to land safely.
Start at the dots.
Trace the broken lines.

37

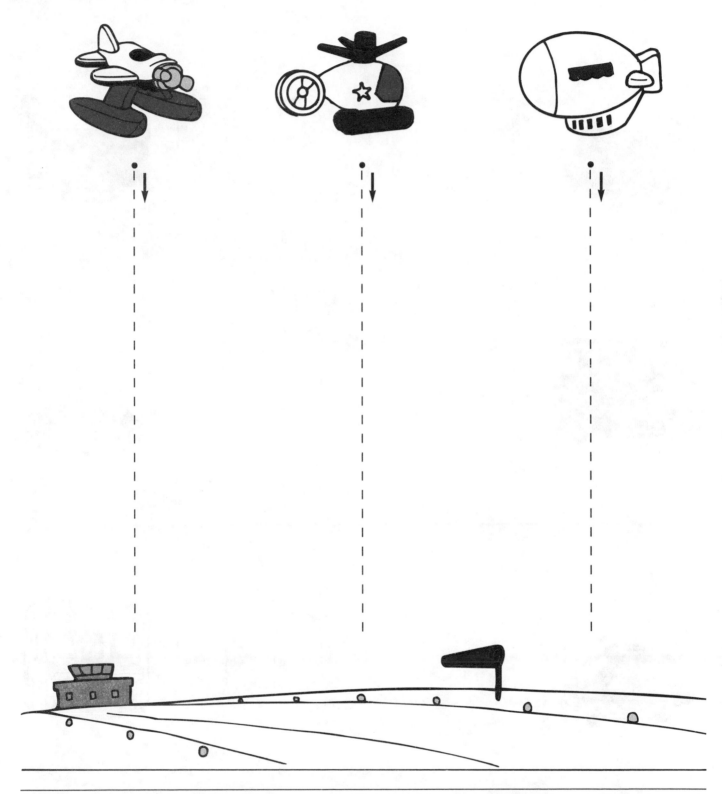

**Skills**: Fine motor skill development; Eye/hand coordination; Forming vertical lines

# IT'S FUN TO BEGIN WRITING

Help each vehicle get to where it's going.
Start at the dots.
Trace the broken lines.

**Skills**: Fine motor skill development; Eye/hand coordination; Forming curves

# IT'S FUN TO BEGIN WRITING

This fellow carries his home on his back.
Trace the broken lines, so you can see him.
Then finish coloring the picture.

Skills: Fine motor skill development; Eye/hand coordination

# IT'S FUN TO BEGIN WRITING

It's time to go to the beach.
What toys will you take?
Trace the broken lines.
Then finish coloring the pictures.

©1997, 2001 Fisher-Price, Inc.

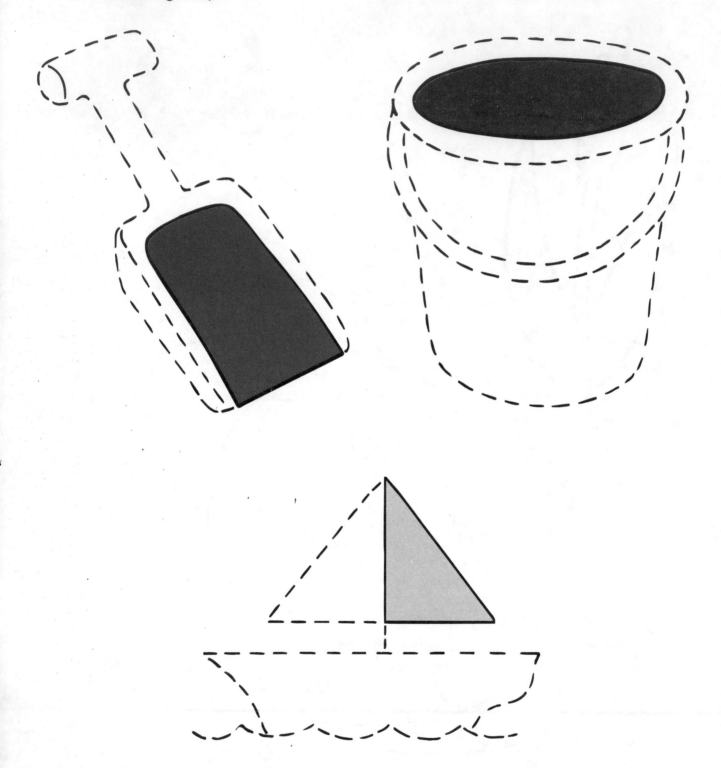

**Skills**: Fine motor skill development; Eye/hand coordination

# IT'S FUN TO BEGIN WRITING

Who followed Little Bo Peep to school?
Connect the dots from **A** to **Z** to find out.
Then finish coloring the picture.

U  T  S  R

Q

V

W

X  P

O

Y  N

Z  M  L

K

A  J

B  I

C

D  H

E  F  G

**Skills**: Fine motor skills; Letter order; Recognition of uppercase letters

# IT'S FUN TO BEGIN WRITING

Who built a house of sticks
that the wolf blew down?
Connect the dots from **a** to **z** to find out.

---

**Skills**: Fine motor skills; Letter order; Recognition of lowercase letters

# IT'S FUN TO BEGIN WRITING

How many letters do you know?
Practice writing the alphabet below.
Trace each letter.
Say each letter. Then, name
something that begins with each letter.

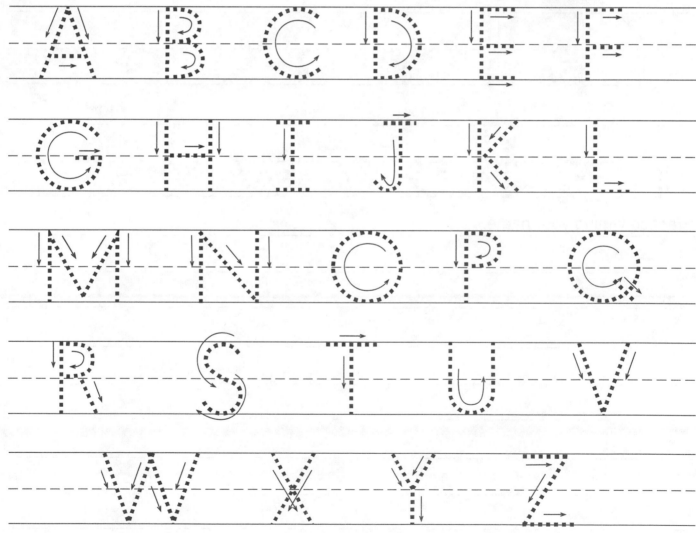

**Skills**: Letter order; Forming uppercase letters; Writing the alphabet; Saying letter sounds; Building vocabulary

# IT'S FUN TO BEGIN WRITING

How many letters do you know?
Practice writing the alphabet below.
Trace each letter.
Say each letter. Then, name
something that begins with each letter.

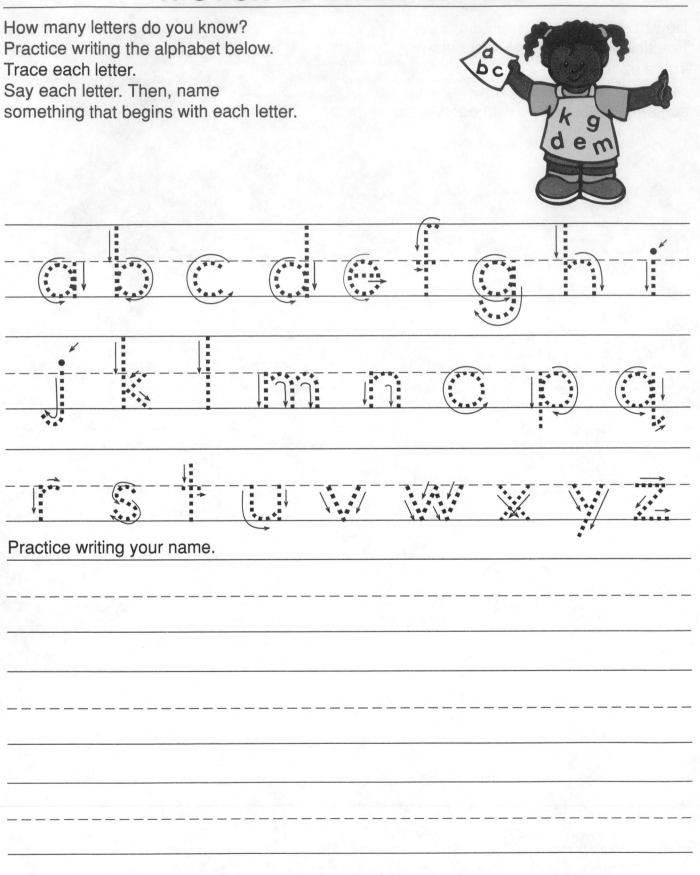

Practice writing your name.

**Skills**: Letter order; Forming lowercase letters; Writing the alphabet; Saying letter sounds; Building vocabulary

# IT'S FUN TO WORK WITH NUMBERS

Trace the number at the beginning of each row.
Then circle that number of things.

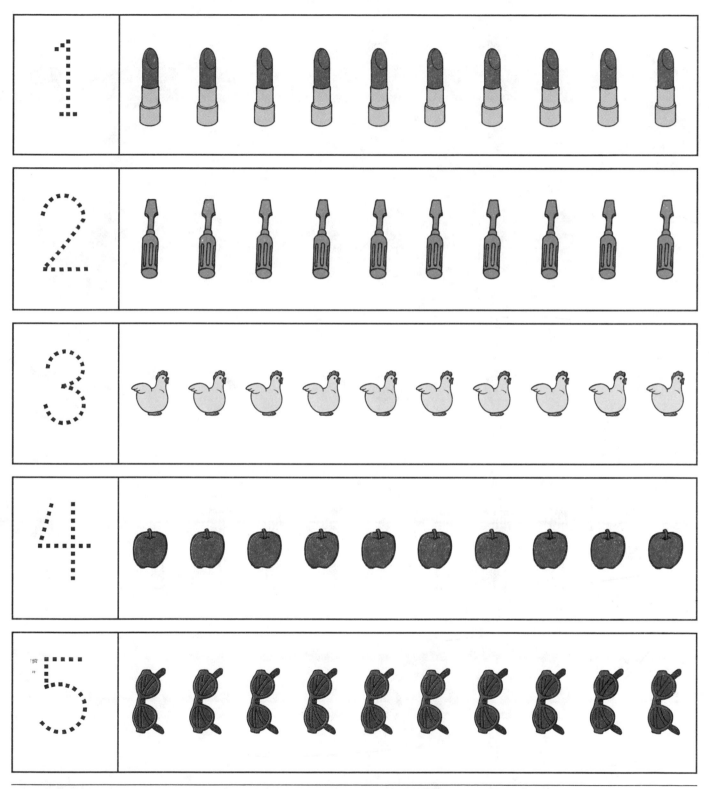

**Skills**: Creating sets of objects; Recognizing numbers; Tracing numbers

# IT'S FUN TO WORK WITH NUMBERS

Trace the number at the beginning of each row.
Then circle that number of things.

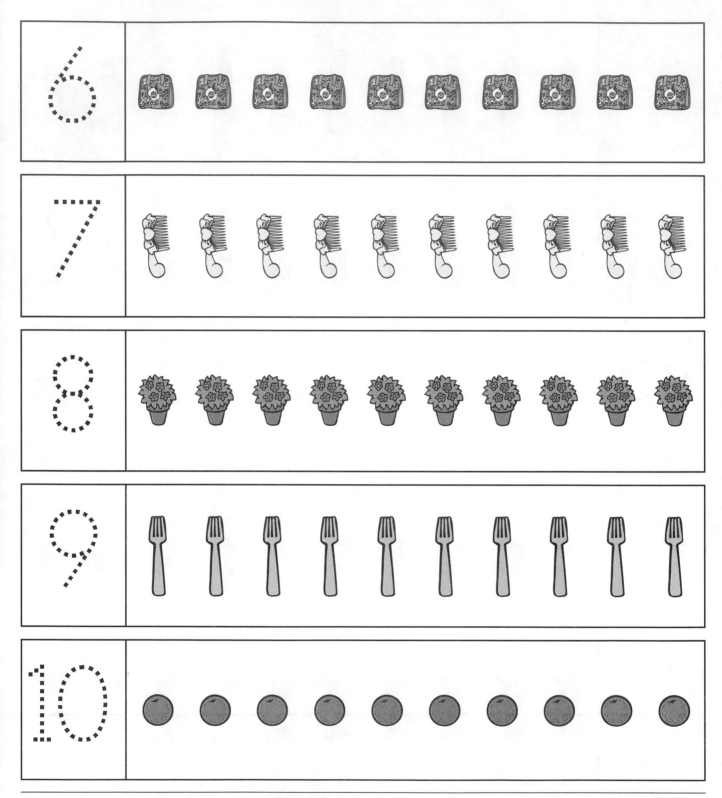

**Skills**: Creating sets of objects; Recognizing numbers; Tracing numbers

# IT'S FUN TO WORK WITH NUMBERS

How many animals do you see in each big box?
Write the number in the small box.

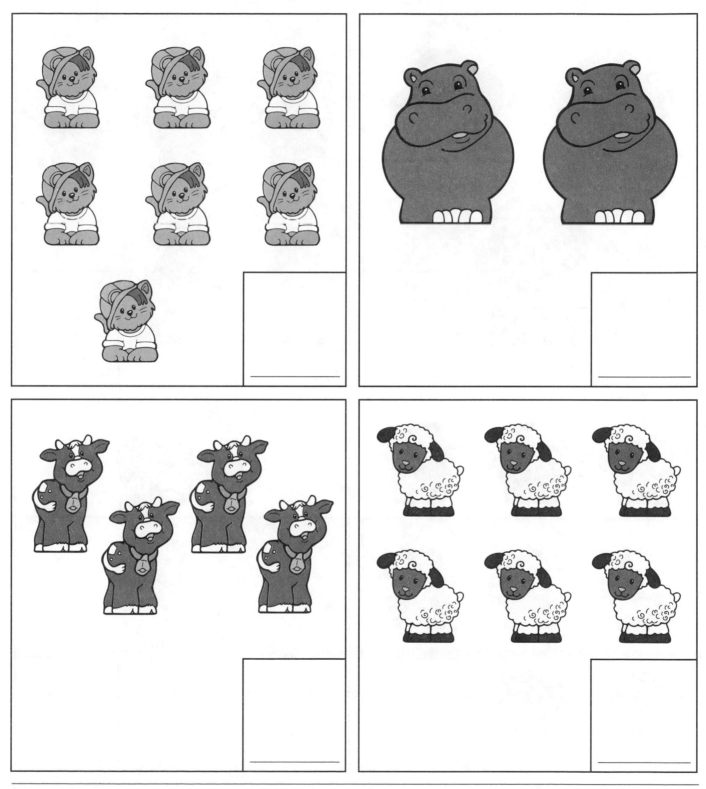

**Skills**: Identifying number sets; Writing numbers

# IT'S FUN TO WORK WITH NUMBERS

How many animals do you see in each big box?
Write the number in the small box.

**Skills**: Identifying number sets; Writing numbers

# IT'S FUN TO WORK WITH NUMBERS

How many animals do you see in each big box?
Write the number in the small box.

**Skills**: Identifying number sets; Writing numbers

# IT'S FUN TO WORK WITH NUMBERS

How many objects are in each set?
Draw a line to connect the sets with the same number of objects.

---

**Skills**: Identifying sets; Matching

# IT'S FUN TO WORK WITH NUMBERS

How many objects are in each set?
Draw a line to connect the sets with the same number of objects.

**Skills**: Identifying sets; Matching

# IT'S FUN TO WORK WITH NUMBERS

Look at the pictures in each box.
Circle the group that shows **less**.

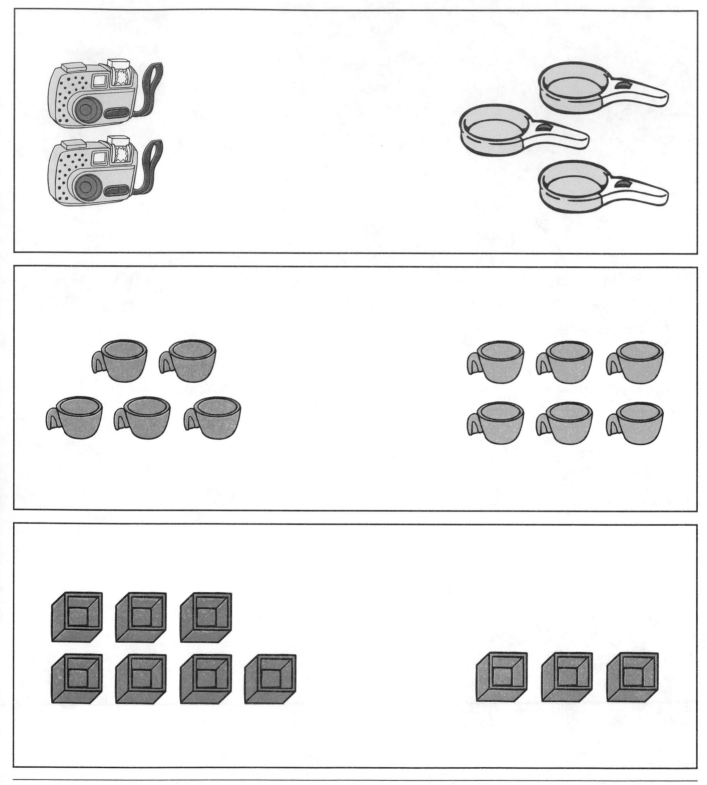

**Skills**: Understanding more and less

# IT'S FUN TO WORK WITH NUMBERS

Look at the pictures in each box.
Circle the group that shows **more**.

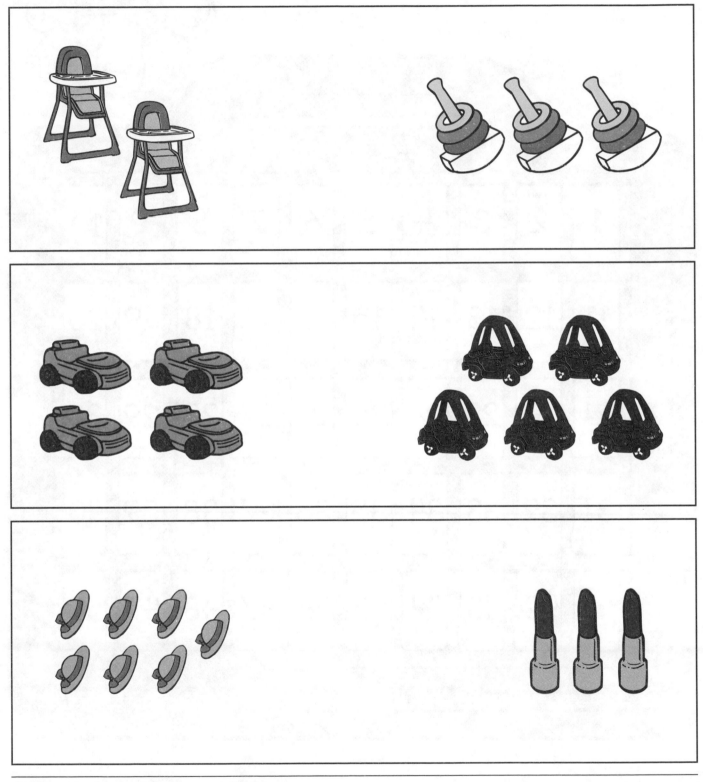

**Skills**: Understanding more and less

# IT'S FUN TO WORK WITH NUMBERS

Point to each number as you count from **1** to **50**.
Circle numbers **12** and **19**.
Put a line under numbers **30** and **40**.
Put an **X** on numbers **15** and **45**.

**Skills**: Counting; Recognizing numbers

# IT'S FUN TO WORK WITH NUMBERS

Bubbles, bubbles everywhere!
How can we make them?
Follow the dots from **1** to **25** to find out.

**Skills**: Number order; Recognizing numbers

# IT'S FUN TO WORK WITH NUMBERS

It's time to rocket into space.
How will we go?
Connect the dots from **1** to **50** to find out.

**Skills**: Number order; Recognizing numbers

# IT'S FUN TO WORK WITH NUMBERS

Say hello to Palace Pony.
Connect the dots from **1** to **50**.

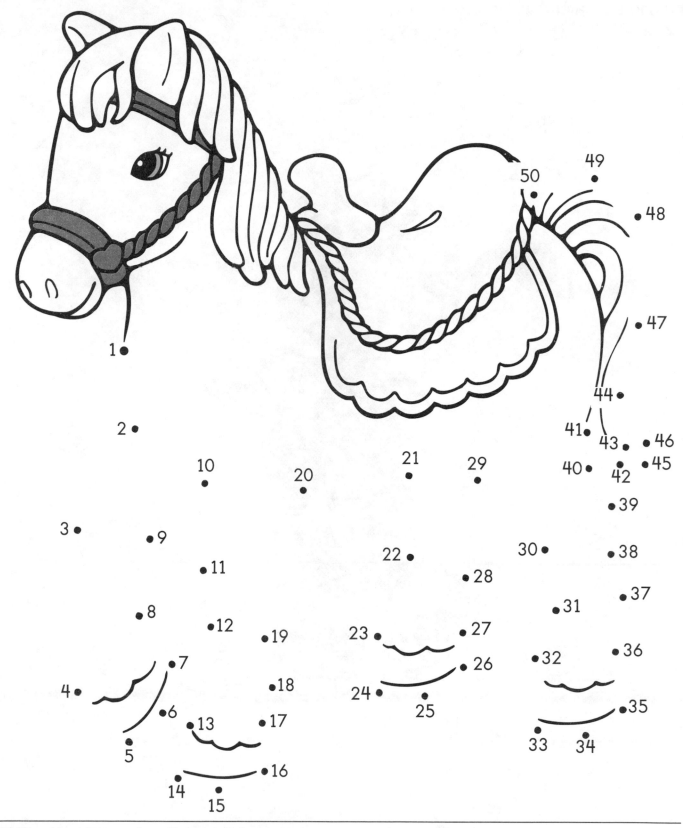

**Skills**: Number order; Recognizing numbers

©1997, 2001 Fisher-Price, Inc.

# IT'S FUN TO WORK WITH NUMBERS

Let's take a swing!
Color all the golf balls that have
numbers greater than **10**.

**Skills**: Comparing numbers

# IT'S FUN TO WORK WITH NUMBERS

Color all the bows
with numbers less than **20**.

**Skills**: Comparing numbers

# IT'S FUN TO WORK WITH NUMBERS

Look closely at this picture.
Find and circle all the things that have numbers.

**Skills**: Recognizing numbers

# IT'S FUN TO WORK WITH NUMBERS

Let's go for a swim!
Look at the large picture below.
Then look at the picture in each small box.
Write the number that tells how many of each object you see.

| **clouds** | **starfish** | **green fish** | **clams** |
|---|---|---|---|

**Skills**: Counting sets of objects; Writing numbers

# IT'S FUN TO WORK WITH NUMBERS

Look at the large picture below.
Then look at the picture in each small box.
Write the number that tells how many of each object you see.

**birds**

**helicopters**

**trees**

**houses**

**Skills**: Counting sets of objects; Writing numbers

# IT'S FUN TO WORK WITH NUMBERS

Sometimes there is less than **1**.
Less than **1** is **zero**.
Trace the **zero**.
Then answer the questions below.

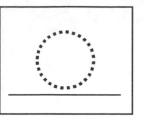
_____

How many keys?

_____

How many keys?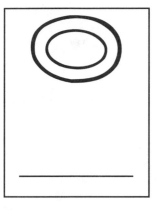

_____

How many pegs?

_____

How many pegs?

_____

How many puppies?

_____

How many puppies?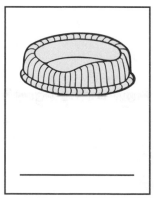

_____

**Skills**: Understanding zero; Counting

# IT'S FUN TO WORK WITH NUMBERS

Sometimes there is less than 1.
Less than 1 is **zero**.
Trace the **zero**.
Then answer the questions below.

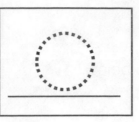

How many bottles?

_____

How many bottles?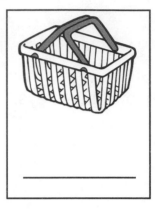

_____

How many books?

_____

How many books?

_____

How many eggs?

_____

How many eggs?

_____

**Skills**: Understanding zero; Counting

# ANSWER KEY

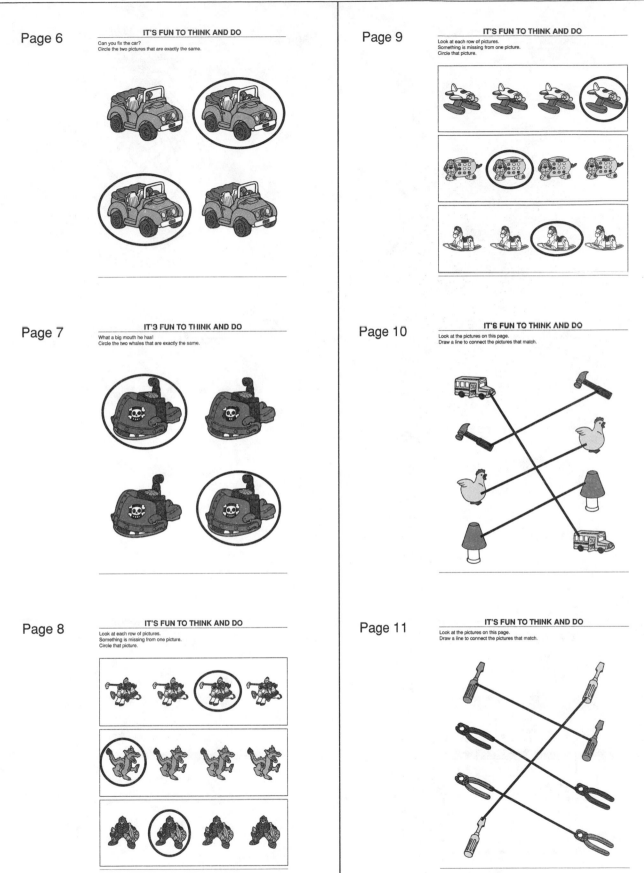

Page 6

**IT'S FUN TO THINK AND DO**
Can you fix the car?
Circle the two pictures that are exactly the same.

Page 7

**IT'S FUN TO THINK AND DO**
What a big mouth he has!
Circle the two whales that are exactly the same.

Page 8

**IT'S FUN TO THINK AND DO**
Look at each row of pictures.
Something is missing from one picture.
Circle that picture.

Page 9

**IT'S FUN TO THINK AND DO**
Look at each row of pictures.
Something is missing from one picture.
Circle that picture.

Page 10

**IT'S FUN TO THINK AND DO**
Look at the pictures on this page.
Draw a line to connect the pictures that match.

Page 11

**IT'S FUN TO THINK AND DO**
Look at the pictures on this page.
Draw a line to connect the pictures that match.

# ANSWER KEY

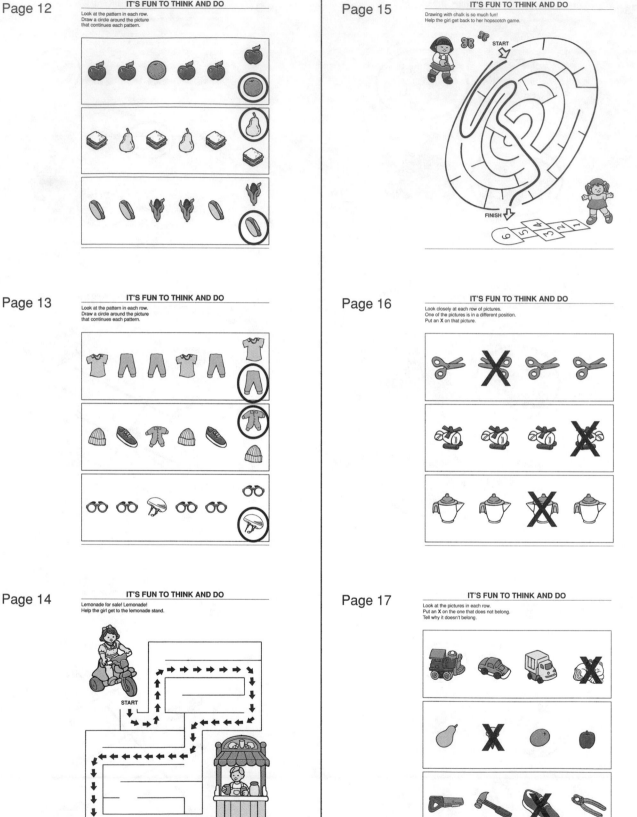

Page 12

**IT'S FUN TO THINK AND DO**

Look at the pattern in each row.
Draw a circle around the picture
that continues each pattern.

Page 13

**IT'S FUN TO THINK AND DO**

Look at the pattern in each row.
Draw a circle around the picture
that continues each pattern.

Page 14

**IT'S FUN TO THINK AND DO**

Lemonade for sale! Lemonade!
Help the girl get to the lemonade stand.

Page 15

**IT'S FUN TO THINK AND DO**

Drawing with chalk is so much fun!
Help the girl get back to her hopscotch game.

Page 16

**IT'S FUN TO THINK AND DO**

Look closely at each row of pictures.
One of the pictures is in a different position.
Put an **X** on that picture.

Page 17

**IT'S FUN TO THINK AND DO**

Look at the pictures in each row.
Put an **X** on the one that does not belong.
Tell why it doesn't belong.

# ANSWER KEY

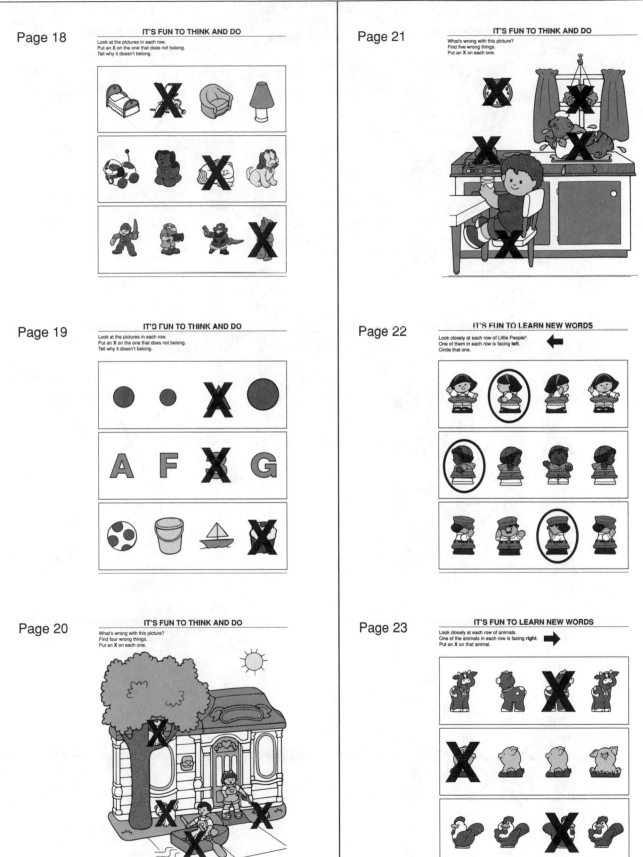

Page 18

**IT'S FUN TO THINK AND DO**
Look at the pictures in each row.
Put an **X** on the one that does not belong.
Tell why it doesn't belong.

Page 19

**IT'S FUN TO THINK AND DO**
Look at the pictures in each row.
Put an **X** on the one that does not belong.
Tell why it doesn't belong.

Page 20

**IT'S FUN TO THINK AND DO**
What's wrong with this picture?
Find four wrong things.
Put an **X** on each one.

Page 21

**IT'S FUN TO THINK AND DO**
What's wrong with this picture?
Find five wrong things.
Put an **X** on each one.

Page 22

**IT'S FUN TO LEARN NEW WORDS**
Look closely at each row of Little People®.
One of them in each row is facing **left**.
Circle that one.

Page 23

**IT'S FUN TO LEARN NEW WORDS**
Look closely at each row of animals.
One of the animals in each row is facing **right**.
Put an **X** on that animal.

# ANSWER KEY

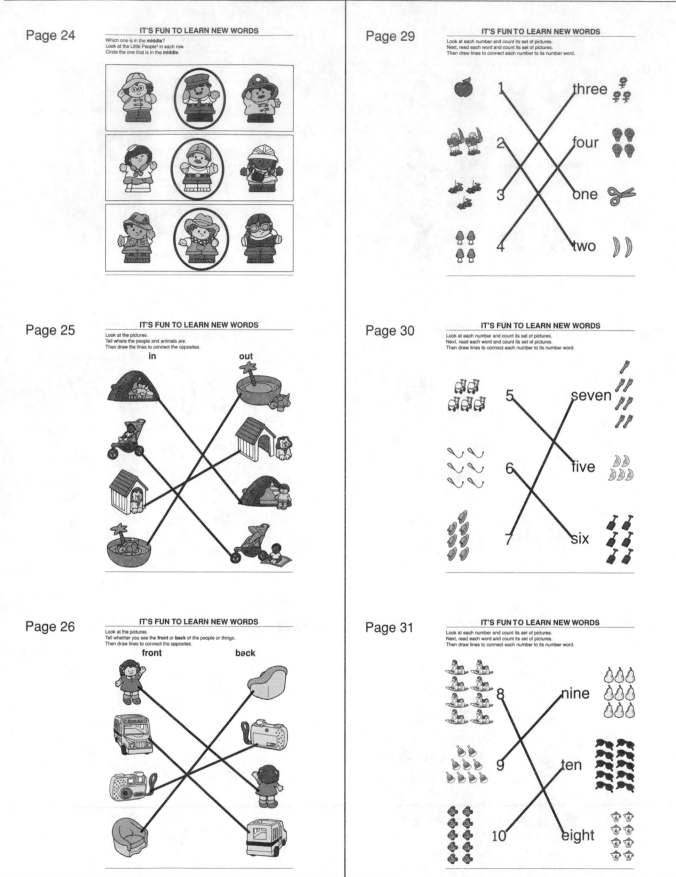

Page 24

**IT'S FUN TO LEARN NEW WORDS**

Which one is in the **middle**?
Look at the Little People® in each row.
Circle the one that is in the **middle**.

Page 25

**IT'S FUN TO LEARN NEW WORDS**

Look at the pictures.
Tell where the people and animals are.
Then draw the lines to connect the opposites.

in     out

Page 26

**IT'S FUN TO LEARN NEW WORDS**

Look at the pictures.
Tell whether you see the **front** or **back** of the people or things.
Then draw lines to connect the opposites.

front     back

Page 29

**IT'S FUN TO LEARN NEW WORDS**

Look at each number and count its set of pictures.
Next, read each word and count its set of pictures.
Then draw lines to connect each number to its number word.

1     three
2     four
3     one
4     two

Page 30

**IT'S FUN TO LEARN NEW WORDS**

Look at each number and count its set of pictures.
Next, read each word and count its set of pictures.
Then draw lines to connect each number to its number word.

5     seven
6     five
7     six

Page 31

**IT'S FUN TO LEARN NEW WORDS**

Look at each number and count its set of pictures.
Next, read each word and count its set of pictures.
Then draw lines to connect each number to its number word.

8     nine
9     ten
10     eight

# ANSWER KEY

**Page 32**

### IT'S FUN TO LEARN NEW WORDS
Look at each color and say its name.
Then draw lines to connect each color word to its matching toy.

red
green
blue
yellow

**Page 33**

### IT'S FUN TO LEARN NEW WORDS
Look at each color and say its name.
Then draw lines to connect each color word to its matching toy.

pink
brown
orange
purple

**Page 41**

### IT'S FUN TO BEGIN WRITING
Who followed Little Bo Peep to school?
Connect the dots from **A** to **Z** to find out.
Then finish coloring the picture.

**Page 42**

### IT'S FUN TO BEGIN WRITING
Who built a house of sticks
that the wolf blew down?
Connect the dots from **a** to **z** to find out.

**Page 45**

### IT'S FUN TO WORK WITH NUMBERS
Trace the number at the beginning of each row.
Then circle that number of things.

1
2
3
4
5

**Page 46**

### IT'S FUN TO WORK WITH NUMBERS
Trace the number at the beginning of each row.
Then circle that number of things.

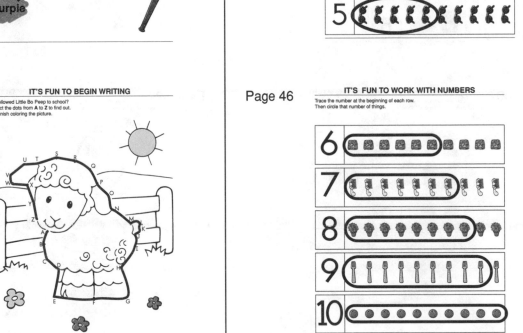

6
7
8
9
10

# ANSWER KEY

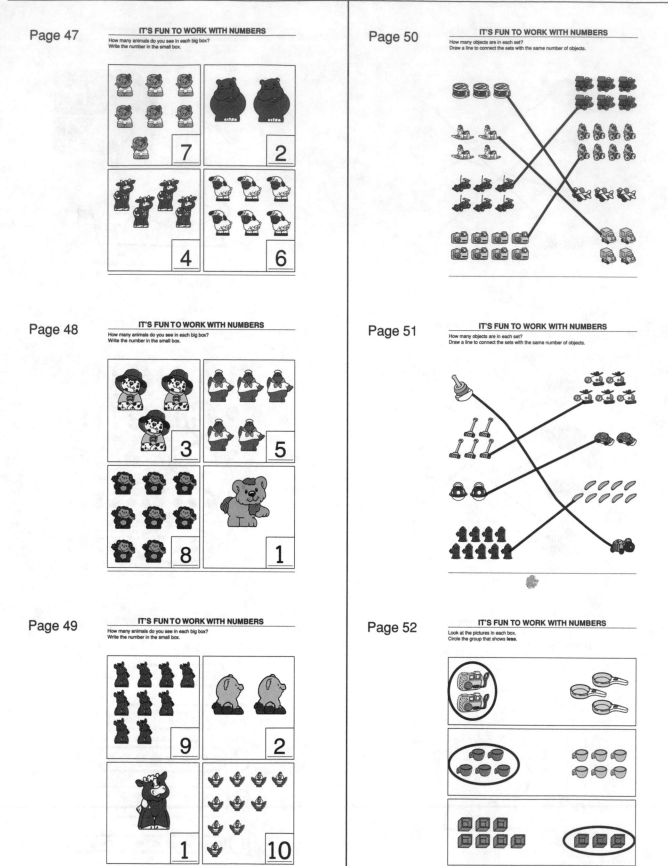

Page 47

**IT'S FUN TO WORK WITH NUMBERS**
How many animals do you see in each big box?
Write the number in the small box.

Page 48

**IT'S FUN TO WORK WITH NUMBERS**
How many animals do you see in each big box?
Write the number in the small box.

Page 49

**IT'S FUN TO WORK WITH NUMBERS**
How many animals do you see in each big box?
Write the number in the small box.

Page 50

**IT'S FUN TO WORK WITH NUMBERS**
How many objects are in each set?
Draw a line to connect the sets with the same number of objects.

Page 51

**IT'S FUN TO WORK WITH NUMBERS**
How many objects are in each set?
Draw a line to connect the sets with the same number of objects.

Page 52

**IT'S FUN TO WORK WITH NUMBERS**
Look at the pictures in each box.
Circle the group that shows **less**.

# ANSWER KEY

Page 53

**IT'S FUN TO WORK WITH NUMBERS**
Look at the pictures in each box.
Circle the group that shows **more**.

Page 54

**IT'S FUN TO WORK WITH NUMBERS**
Point to each number as you count from 1 to **50**.
Circle numbers **12** and **19**.
Put a line under numbers **30** and **40**.
Put an **X** on numbers **15** and **45**.

Page 55

**IT'S FUN TO WORK WITH NUMBERS**
Bubbles, bubbles everywhere!
How can we make them?
Follow the dots from 1 to **25** to find out.

Page 56

**IT'S FUN TO WORK WITH NUMBERS**
It's time to rocket into space.
How will we go?
Connect the dots from **1** to **50** to find out.

Page 57

**IT'S FUN TO WORK WITH NUMBERS**
Say hello to Palace Pony.
Connect the dots from 1 to **50**.

Page 58

**IT'S FUN TO WORK WITH NUMBERS**
Let's take a swing!
Color all the golf balls that have
numbers greater than **10**.

# ANSWER KEY

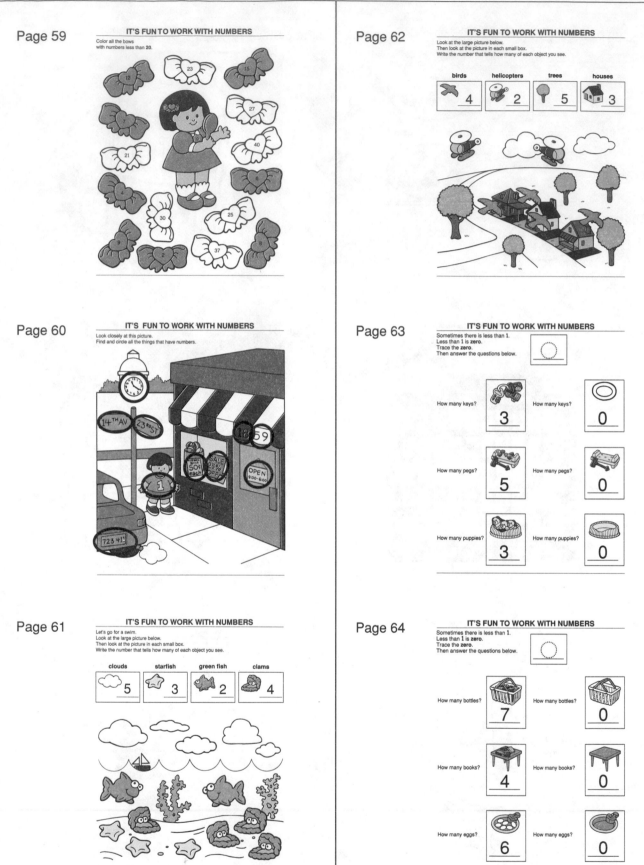

**Page 59**

IT'S FUN TO WORK WITH NUMBERS
Color all the bows
with numbers less than **20**.

12  23  15
27
21  40
4  6
30  25
9  2  37  8

**Page 60**

IT'S FUN TO WORK WITH NUMBERS
Look closely at this picture.
Find and circle all the things that have numbers.

**Page 61**

IT'S FUN TO WORK WITH NUMBERS
Let's go for a swim.
Look at the large picture below.
Then look at the picture in each small box.
Write the number that tells how many of each object you see.

| clouds | starfish | green fish | clams |
|--------|----------|-----------|-------|
| 5 | 3 | 2 | 4 |

**Page 62**

IT'S FUN TO WORK WITH NUMBERS
Look at the large picture below.
Then look at the picture in each small box.
Write the number that tells how many of each object you see.

| birds | helicopters | trees | houses |
|-------|-------------|-------|--------|
| 4 | 2 | 5 | 3 |

**Page 63**

IT'S FUN TO WORK WITH NUMBERS
Sometimes there is less than 1.
Less than 1 is **zero**.
Trace the **zero**.
Then answer the questions below.

How many keys? 3   How many keys? 0

How many pegs? 5   How many pegs? 0

How many puppies? 3   How many puppies? 0

**Page 64**

IT'S FUN TO WORK WITH NUMBERS
Sometimes there is less than 1.
Less than 1 is **zero**.
Trace the **zero**.
Then answer the questions below.

How many bottles? 7   How many bottles? 0

How many books? 4   How many books? 0

How many eggs? 6   How many eggs? 0